# 101 Uplifting Quotes About Change

## When You Need a Little Push Before Taking a Big Leap in Your Life

## Phil Collins

## Copyright © 2023 Phil Collins

# Table of Contents


**Dedication**

**Introduction**

**101 Uplifting Quotes About Change**

**Closing Remark**

# Dedication

To those embracing change's transformative dance, may these uplifting quotes be your guiding light as you embark on the journey of transformation. This book is dedicated to the courageous souls chasing dreams, embracing evolution, and finding strength in every shift.

# Introduction

These quotations about transformation can be just what you need at this point in your life.

There will always be change. The statements about change that follows demonstrate how change may sometimes come at you quickly and forcefully and other times gradually.

One big incident may cause a tremendous alteration, or you may see over time that things have changed. There's usually a bright side to these adjustments, whether they're beneficial and essential or not at the moment.

Naturally, adapting to change is seldom simple. Many of us would want to escape the suffering that might result from losing someone we care about or from going through challenging personal development in general.

Many of us would want to avoid the discomfort of experiencing a changed relationship or the difficult portion of beginning anything new (like a job) and instead go straight to the point when we are already used to the new setting, updated friendship dynamics, etc. But the process is enjoyable!

These encouraging sayings about change are all about evolving, taking risks, and trying new things.

See these 101 quotes on change to be inspired and encouraged to see the positive side of things during a period of significant upheaval, or if you could use some assistance making sense of a confusing and turbulent moment.

# 101 Uplifting Quotes About Change

1. "Change, like healing, takes time."
— **Veronica Roth**




2. "If I am not for myself, who will be for me? But if I am only for myself, what am I? And if not now, when?
- **Hillel**

3. "Things change. And friends leave. Life doesn't stop for anybody."
— **Stephen Chbosky**

4. "Everyone thinks of changing the world, but no one thinks of changing himself."
— **Leo Tolstoy**

5. "Those who cannot change their minds cannot change anything."
— **George Bernard Shaw**

6. "I alone cannot change the world, but I can cast a stone across the waters to create many ripples."
— **Mother Teresa**

7. "Change will not come if we wait for some other person, or if we wait for some other time. We are the ones we've been waiting for. We are the change that we seek."
— **Barack Obama**

8. "The world as we have created it is a process of our thinking. It cannot be changed without changing our thinking."
— **Albert Einstein**

9. "To change one's life: 1. Start immediately. 2. Do it flamboyantly. 3. No exceptions."
**— William James**

10. "Yesterday I was clever, so I wanted to change the world. Today I am wise, so I am changing myself."
**— Rumi**

11. "I don't need a friend who changes when
I change and who nods when I nod; my
shadow does that much better"
**- Plutarch**

12. "Nothing is so painful to the human
mind as a great and sudden change."
**— Mary Shelley**

13. "Life is a series of natural and spontaneous changes. Don't resist them; that only creates sorrow. Let reality be reality. Let things flow naturally forward in whatever way they like."
— **Lao Tzu**

14. "Incredible change happens in your life when you decide to take control of what you do have power over instead of craving control over what you don't."
**- Steve Maraboli**

15. "I have accepted fear as part of life –
specifically the fear of change... I have gone
ahead despite the pounding in the heart that
says: turn back...."
**— Erica Jong**


16. "We are not trapped or locked up in
these bones. No, no. We are free to change.
And love changes us. And if we can love one
another, we can break open the sky."
**— Walter Mosley**

17. "Change the way you look at things and the things you look at change."
— **Wayne W. Dyer**

18. "Taking a new step, uttering a new word, is what people fear most."
— **Fyodor Dostoevsky,** Crime and Punishment

19. "You're always you, and that don't change, and you're always changing, and there's nothing you can do about it."
— **Neil Gaiman,** The Graveyard Book

20. "And that is how change happens. One gesture. One person. One moment at a time."
— **Libba Bray,** The Sweet Far Thing

21. "Some changes look negative on the surface but you will soon realize that space is being created in your life for something new to emerge."
— **Eckhart Tolle**

22. "Certain things, they should stay the way they are. You ought to be able to stick them in one of those big glass cases and just leave them alone."
— **J.D. Salinger**, The Catcher in the Rye

23. "Believe something and the Universe is on its way to being changed. Because you've changed, by believing. Once you've changed, other things start to follow. Isn't that the way it works?"
— **Diane Duane**

24. "Maturity is when you stop complaining and making excuses, and start making changes."
— **Roy T. Bennett**

25. "Fashion changes, but style endures."
— **Coco Chanel**

26. "You never change things by fighting the existing reality. To change something, build a new model that makes the existing model obsolete."
— **Buckminster Fuller**

27. "You cannot change what you are, only
what you do."
— **Philip Pullman**




28. "Faced with the choice between
changing one's mind and proving that there
is no need to do so, almost everyone gets
busy on the proof."
- **John Kenneth Galbraith**

29. "Time takes it all, whether you want it to or not."
— **Stephen King,** The Green Mile

30. "No matter who you are, no matter what you did, no matter where you've come from, you can always change, become a better version of yourself."
— **Madonna**

31. "The philosophers have only interpreted
the world, in various ways. The point,
however, is to change it."
**– Karl Marx**

32. "I find the best way to love somcone is
not to change them, but instead, help them
reveal the greatest version of themselves."
**— Steve Maraboli**

33. "All that you touch
You Change.
All that you Change
Changes you.
The only lasting truth
is Change.
God is Change."
— **Octavia E. Butler**




34. "Every woman that finally figured out
her worth, has picked up her suitcases of
pride and boarded a flight to freedom, which
landed in the valley of change."
— **Shannon L. Alder**

35. "Anger, resentment and jealousy doesn't change the heart of others-- it only changes yours."
— **Shannon Alder**

36. "If you're in a bad situation, don't worry it'll change. If you're in a good situation, don't worry it'll change."
— **John A. Simone, Sr.**

37. "One child, one teacher, one book, one pen can change the world."
— **Malala Yousafzai**

38. "When people are ready to, they change. They never do it before then, and sometimes they die before they get around to it. You can't make them change if they don't want to, just like when they do want to, you can't stop them."
— **Andy Warhol**

39. "No one can tell what goes on in between the person you were and the person you become. No one can chart that blue and lonely section of hell. There are no maps of the change. You just come out the other side. Or you don't."
— **Stephen King, The Stand**

40. "Vulnerability is the birthplace of innovation, creativity and change."
— **Brene Brown**

41. "To improve is to change; to be perfect is to change often."
— **Winston S. Churchill**

42. "Desperation is the raw material of drastic change. Only those who can leave behind everything they have ever believed in can hope to escape. "
— **William S. Burroughs**

43. "When you come out of the storm, you won't be the same person who walked in. That's what this storm's all about."
— **Haruki Murakami**


44. "The people who are crazy enough to think they can change the world are the ones who do."
— **Steve Jobs**

45. "I give you this to take with you: Nothing remains as it was. If you know this, you can begin again, with pure joy in the uprooting."
— **Judith Minty**




46. "A bend in the road is not the end of the road... Unless you fail to make the turn."
— **Helen Keller**

47. "Life belongs to the living, and he who
lives must be prepared for changes."
**— Johann Wolfgang von Goethe**

48. "Change may not always bring growth,
but there is no growth without change."
**— Roy T. Bennett**

49. "True life is lived when tiny changes occur."
— **Leo Tolstoy**


50. "Change begins at the end of your comfort zone."
— **Roy T. Bennett**

51. "Change is the end result of all true learning."
— **Leo Buscaglia**

52. "Our ability to adapt is amazing. Our ability to change isn't quite as spectacular."
— **Lisa Lutz**

53. "Changing is what people do when they
have no options left."
— **Holly Black**


54. "To change ourselves effectively, we first
had to change our perceptions."
— **Stephen R. Covey**

55. "Nothing is lost . . . Everything is
transformed."
— **Michael Ende**




56. "The changes we dread most may
contain our salvation."
— **Barbara Kingsolver**

57. "If you want to change attitudes, start with a change in behavior."
— **Katherine Hepburn**

58. "It's not that some people have willpower and some don't... It's that some people are ready to change and others are not."
— **James Gordon**

59. "You tried to change didn't you? Closed your mouth more, tried to be softer, prettier, less volatile, less awake... You can't make homes out of human beings. Someone should have already told you that."
— **Warsan Shire**

60. "Don't knock the weather; nine-tenths of the people couldn't start a conversation if it didn't change once in a while."
— **Kin Hubbard**

61. "Change your thoughts and you change
your world."
— **Norman Vincent Peale**




62. "Nothing endures but change."
— **Heraclitus**

63. "The past can teach us, nurture us, but it cannot sustain us. The essence of life is change, and we must move ever forward or the soul will wither and die."
— **Susanna Kearsley**

64. "Anyone who isn't embarrassed of who they were last year probably isn't learning enough."
— **Alain de Botton**

65. "If you want to make enemies, try to
change something."
**- Woodrow Wilson**

66. "The only difference between a rut and a
grave is their dimensions."
**- Ellen Glasgow**

67. "People are very open-minded about new things, as long as they're exactly like the old ones."
- **Charles F. Kettering**




68. "The great growling engine of change — technology."
— **Alvin Toffler**

69. "Folks, I don't trust children. They're here to replace us."
— **Stephen Colbert**

70. "No matter what people will tell you, words and ideas can change the world."
— **Robin Williams**

71. "People change for two reasons; either they learned a lot or they've been hurt too much."
**– Unknown**

72. "The secret of change is to focus all of your energy, not on fighting the old, but on building the new."
**– Socrates**

73. "Act the way you'd like to be and soon
you'll be the way you'd like to act."
— **Bob Dylan**


74. "Change your life today. Don't gamble on
the future, act now, without delay."
— **Simone de Beauvoir**

75. "Change is hardest at the beginning, messiest in the middle and best at the end."
— **Robin Sharma**

76. "And all the lives we ever lived and all the lives to be are full of trees and changing leaves."
— **Virginia Woolf**, To the Lighthouse

77. "We first make our habits, then our habits make us."
— **John Dryden**

78. "Words are where most change begins."
— **Brandon Sanderson**

79. "People who can change and change again are so much more reliable and happier than those who can't"
— **Stephen Fry**

80. "What people have the capacity to choose, they have the ability to change."
— **Madeleine Albright**

81. "If we don't change, we don't grow. If we don't grow, we aren't really living."
— **Anatole France**

82. "People can cry much easier than they can change."
— **James Baldwin**

83. "Change almost never fails because it's too early. It almost always fails because it's too late."
— **Seth Godin**

84. "People don't change, they just have momentary steps outside of their true character."
— **Chad Kultgen**

85. "Every hundred feet the world changes."
— **Roberto Bolaño**

86. "Consider how hard it is to change
yourself and you'll understand what little
chance you have in trying to change others."
— **Jacob M. Braude**

87. "I wanted change and excitement and to shoot off in all directions myself, like the colored arrows from a Fourth of July rocket."
— **Sylvia Plath**

88. "What is necessary to change a person is to change his awareness of himself."
— **Abraham Maslow**

89. "It was long since I had longed for anything and the effect on me was horrible."
— **Samuel Beckett**

90. "All is flux, nothing stays still."
— **Plato**

91. "People don't resist change. They resist being changed."
— **Peter Senge**

92. "Sometimes you hit a point where you either change or self-destruct."
— **Sam Stevens**

93. "Either way, change will come. It could be bloody, or it could be beautiful. It depends on us."
— **Arundhati Roy**

94. "We change the world not by what we say or do, but as a consequence of what we have become."
— **Dr. David Hawkins**

95. "The struggles we endure today will be the 'good old days' we laugh about tomorrow."
— **Aaron Lauritsen**

96. "Bending beats breaking."
— **Betty Greene**

97. "The world doesn't change in front of your eyes, it changes behind your back."
— **Terry Hayes**

98. "Man cannot remake himself without suffering, for he is both the marble and the sculptor"
— **Alexis Carrel**

99. "Tides do what tides do–they turn."
— **Derek Landy**


100. "The greatest discovery of all time is
that a person can change his future by
merely changing his attitude."
— **Oprah Winfrcy**

101. "Only the wisest and stupidest of men
never change."
— **Confucius**

# Closing Remark

May these pages be a source of inspiration and encouragement as you navigate the winds of change.

Embrace each moment, seize every opportunity, and remember, your resilience amidst change shapes the masterpiece of your life.

Here's to a journey filled with growth, courage, and endless possibilities.